Contents

Criminal behaviour 4

The "Dan Cooper" hijacking 6

The Northern Bank robbery 10

The Isabella Stewart Gardner
Museum heist 14

The Lloyds Bank robbery 18

Pill poisonings 22

The Springfield Three 24

Amsterdam diamond heist 26

Glossary 30
Books 31
Websites 31
Index 32

Criminal behaviour

Some criminals are really easy to catch – especially when they use social media. One bank robber in Nebraska, USA, boasted about her crime on YouTube. Police tracked her down pretty quickly thanks to the photos she provided. Then there were four bank robbers in Texas, USA, who got caught after posting details about their crime on Facebook. It didn't take long for police to arrest them.

A thief in Cambridge got caught the old-fashioned way. After breaking into a house, he decided to take a nap. The owner of the house came home, found him on the sofa and called the police. Case closed.

DO NOT CROSS

CRIME SCENE

Of course, most criminals are harder to find. In fact, many get away with their crimes for a while. It takes a mistake or good police work to put them in prison. And then there are some criminals who seem to pull off the perfect crimes. They leave the police baffled.

Perhaps it's because the criminals are clever. Or perhaps it's because they take huge risks. It may be both of those advantages mixed with some luck. These daring crimes can capture the public's imagination. They leave us asking: "How did they do it?" or "Why did they do it?" and "Could it happen again?"

CRIME SCENE
DO NOT CROSS

The "Dan Cooper" hijacking

On 24 November 1971, a man went down in history for the most daring escape ever. Dan Cooper **hijacked** an aeroplane in Washington, USA, and received a huge **ransom**. After releasing all of the passengers, he demanded that the pilots fly the plane to Mexico.

But then Cooper did something shocking – he parachuted out of the plane. The conditions for skydiving were awful. It was cold and rainy. Cooper was jumping into the wooded mountains of the Pacific Northwest.

Cooper has never been caught. Did he survive, and disappear into the dense woods? Is his body still waiting to be found? Either way, Cooper's hijacking is one of the greatest unsolved crimes of all time.

hijack take illegal control of a vehicle, such as an aeroplane

ransom money or objects that are demanded in order to set free someone who is being held captive

Who is Dan Cooper?

The hijacker used the **alias** "Dan Cooper". But newspapers mistakenly reported his name as "D.B. Cooper", so most people remember him by that name. Investigators know almost nothing about Cooper. But they do know that he boarded a plane in Oregon, USA, that night. The flight to Seattle appeared to be routine. During the flight nobody really noticed Cooper.

Then Cooper took over the Boeing 727. He said he had a bomb and that he'd kill all of the passengers and crew if they didn't do what he asked. He demanded four parachutes and $200,000 in $20 bills. That amount is worth about £1.6 million today.

alias false name, especially one used by a criminal

The jump

The plane landed in Washington. Cooper released the passengers, but not the pilots. As demanded, the Federal Bureau of Investigation (FBI) gave Cooper the parachutes and money. Cooper then ordered the pilots to fly to Mexico. Shortly after, Cooper made his famous jump into the night. Even though police were following in other aeroplanes, they didn't see Cooper jump or where he landed.

Did Cooper survive?

Few people believe Cooper survived the jump out of the plane. It's unlikely that he landed safely in such a heavily wooded area. Even if he did, his light clothing would not have protected him from the freezing temperatures for long. If Cooper is still alive today, he has succeeded in one of the most daring crimes of all time.

One solid clue

The huge manhunt that followed Cooper's hijacking turned up almost no evidence. But in 1980 a boy playing near the Columbia River in Oregon found $5,800 (about £3,700) in $20 bills. The **serial numbers** on the bills matched the money that Cooper had with him. A search of the area also uncovered a skull. But it was the skull of a woman, not Cooper.

FBI agents looked for clues along the Columbia River, after some of the ransom money was discovered there in 1980.

serial number number that identifies a product, such as money or an appliance

The Northern Bank robbery

Just before Christmas in 2004, gang members in Belfast, Northern Ireland, pulled off a daring **heist**. On 19 December, armed men posed as police officers to gain entry into two homes. One belonged to Chris Ward; the other belonged to Kevin McMullan. Both men were executives at Northern Bank.

Thieves held the two families at gunpoint. Ward was taken to McMullan's house. Meanwhile McMullan's wife was taken to a forest south of Belfast. All of the family members remained **hostages**. Ward and McMullan were told to go into work the following day and behave normally. If they tipped off anyone, their families would be killed.

Both men cooperated. At the end of the day, the two men led the thieves into the bank's underground **vault**. Both men had been selected because they had keys to the vault, and two keys were needed to get in. The thieves got away with about £26 million in cash. It was the biggest all-cash robbery in UK history.

heist armed robbery

hostage person held against his or her will

vault room or compartment for keeping money and other valuables safe

Leaving few clues behind

The men involved knew exactly what to do to leave behind as little evidence as possible, including shaving off facial hair. They did this to avoid leaving behind anything that could provide DNA evidence to police. DNA is a type of molecule that makes up each person's body. Most DNA molecules are unique. DNA evidence can be matched up to a certain person to help prove that he or she committed a crime.

Newspaper headlines alerted the public to the Northern Bank heist shortly after the crime.

The hostages

None of the hostages were killed. But they all suffered during the heist. McMullan's wife, Karyn, suffered the most. She had no warm clothing or shoes. She was also blindfolded for nearly 24 hours. But she managed to escape and alert police.

Who did it?

Suspicion immediately fell on the Provisional Irish Republican Army (Provisional IRA). The Provisional IRA was a violent resistance group that wanted Northern Ireland to break away from the UK and join Ireland. The organization had a long history of violent robberies and kidnappings to fund its operations. The Northern Bank robbery was carried out so professionally that almost everyone assumed that the Provisional IRA was involved.

A threat to peace

The Northern Bank robbery was one of several crimes blamed on the Provisional IRA. Some members of the IRA have also been accused of murders and spying. Shortly before the robbery, however, the IRA had announced it would end its armed campaign.

Inside job?

Northern Bank regularly changed the people who had the keys to its vault. Whoever carried out the robbery knew exactly which two executives to target. It appeared the robbers had inside information. Who gave this information to the criminals? In 2008 Chris Ward was put on trial for being the "inside man". But the case quickly fell apart after little evidence was found. The **identity** of the thieves remains a mystery.

identity who a person is

The Isabella Stewart Gardner
Museum heist

In the early hours of 18 March 1990, thieves disguised as police officers entered Boston's Isabella Stewart Gardner Museum in the United States. Their disguises fooled the two security guards, who were quickly tied up. The thieves then made off with millions of dollars worth of valuable objects from the museum.

The stolen objects weren't just any works of art. They included 13 paintings and other objects made by world-famous masters such as Rembrandt and Vermeer. Then the thieves and the artworks disappeared. However, the works of art were so well known that they couldn't simply be sold to any buyer. The thieves must have known someone who would buy the artworks in advance. Or perhaps they wanted to keep the works themselves. Either way, the thieves have **eluded** capture for more than 25 years.

elude escape or get away from someone

To catch a thief

In 2013, FBI agents reported they knew the identity of the thieves. FBI agents stated that the thieves were tied to a criminal organization based in the north-eastern United States. Even if caught, however, the criminals can no longer be arrested for the thefts. No legal action can now take place because too much time has passed. The criminals could be arrested for possessing stolen property. But authorities say they will not press charges if the artwork is returned voluntarily.

Are they OK?

Officials at the Gardner Museum publicly urge the thieves to take care of the works. Old paintings can be especially **fragile** if not kept under the right conditions. Officials also worry that those who have the stolen artworks could destroy them on purpose to protect themselves from criminal charges.

The artwork stolen from the Gardner Museum is believed to be worth about £191 million. But such famous works of art cannot be replaced. So, in reality, the stolen works are priceless.

The Gardner Museum has not replaced the works of art on its gallery walls. Instead it has left gaps where the works once were.

The Lloyds Bank robbery

In 1971, a group of thieves set out to break into Lloyds Bank in London. Their goal was to get to the bank's most secure room. This room contained safe deposit boxes. Safe deposit boxes are where people store their most valuable possessions for safety. Often these boxes hold diamonds, jewellery and large amounts of cash.

EXIT TO BANK
23 x 38 CENTIMETRES

LENGTH 12 METRE

BANK BASEMENT
SOLID CONCRETE

10524   10574

10525

10526

10527

The thieves' plan for getting into the room was clever and dangerous. They were going to tunnel under the bank and break in through the floor. In order to do that, they had to rent a shop two doors away, close it down and start the tunnel there. In addition to this, they had to tunnel under a restaurant between the shop and the bank. They could only dig on Sundays when all the shops were closed, to avoid being heard.

The work took months. But when the gang finally did get in, they made off with **loot** worth nearly £32 million in today's money. It was one of the boldest bank robberies ever.

TUNNEL ENTRANCE
46 x 46 CENTIMETRES

ENTRANCE
DEPTH 1.5 METRES

The rented shop was close to the bank, allowing the criminals to gain underground access.

loot stolen money or valuables

19

Walkie-talkie chatter

The thieves put a lookout on a nearby roof and communicated with **walkie-talkies** during the robbery. A radio operator close by overheard their talk and realized what was happening. He called the police. The police should have been able to work out which bank was being robbed. But they decided to search too large an area, so the thieves got away.

Who committed the crime?

Police found four men connected to the crime, because of a foolish mistake. One of the men had used his real name when renting the shop where the tunnel started. Police immediately looked for known criminal **associates**. The rest of the thieves were soon arrested and imprisoned for the robbery.

But their arrest raised many questions. All of them had been "small-time" thieves. None of them had ever shown the skills needed to dig tunnels. None had ever used heavy equipment or explosives. All of those skills were needed for the Lloyds Bank robbery. Because of that, many police officers believed others were involved, or that a criminal **mastermind** was behind it. But nobody else has ever been caught.

Safe deposit boxes at Lloyds Bank held people's important valuables, such as money and jewellery. None of the loot from the robbery has ever been found or returned to its rightful owners.

10524

10531

10532

walkie-talkie radio that is held in the hand, powered by batteries and used to communicate over short distances

associate person you spend time with or work with

mastermind person who plans and controls the way an action is carried out

21

Pill poisonings

On 29 September 1982, 12-year-old Mary Kellerman's parents gave her a paracetamol called Extra-Strength Tylenol to help her feel better. But the capsules held a deadly ingredient. Someone had added small amounts of a poison called cyanide to the bottle. Within the next few days, six other people were poisoned in the same way. Four of them, including Mary, died. All of them lived near Chicago, USA.

People around the world panicked. Nobody felt safe taking bottled medicines. Millions threw away their Tylenol and other pills. Tylenol was taken off the shelves of shops and chemists.

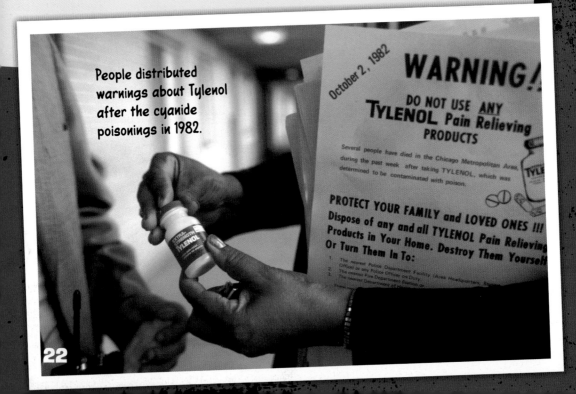

People distributed warnings about Tylenol after the cyanide poisonings in 1982.

October 2, 1982

WARNING!

DO NOT USE ANY
TYLENOL Pain Relieving
PRODUCTS

Several people have died in the Chicago Metropolitan Area, during the past week after taking TYLENOL, which was determined to be contaminated with poison.

PROTECT YOUR FAMILY and LOVED ONES !!!
Dispose of any and all TYLENOL Pain Relieving Products in Your Home. Destroy Them Yourself Or Turn Them In To:

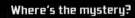

Ongoing investigation

Police cars in the Chicago area drove up and down streets, warning people over loudspeakers not to use Tylenol. Despite a huge police search, no killer was ever found.

One man wrote a ransom note demanding money to stop the poisonings. He was caught, but police soon discovered that he could not have committed the poisonings. Others were investigated, too, but no clear answer has ever been found. Nobody knows why the poisonings took place.

Big changes

In the United States, bottled pills such as Tylenol were packaged differently after the 1982 incident. Food and drug makers came up with **tamper**-proof packages with seals. The new packaging made it much more difficult for someone to add poison or other dangerous substances to pill bottles.

tamper interfere with something so that it becomes damaged or broken

23

The Springfield Three

On 7 June 1992, Stacy McCall, Suzanne "Suzie" Streeter and Suzie's mother, Sherrill Levitt, vanished from Levitt's home in Springfield, Missouri, USA. The three women haven't been seen since.

Friends and neighbours did not realize that they had disappeared until the following day. Stacy and Suzie were supposed to meet up with friends. They had just **graduated** from high school and were supposed to go to several parties. Friends came looking for them when they didn't arrive. All of the women's personal property – including bags, cars and keys – were still at home. Stacy's mum called the police.

Where are they?

The three disappearances remain a mystery. There have been several **suspects**. The lead suspect for a short time was Robert Craig Cox. He is a convicted kidnapper who is also suspected of murder. Cox, who is in prison for another crime, has hinted that he knows what happened to the women. But police fear Cox lied just to get attention. Police assume that the three women were murdered. But no bodies have ever been found.

A poster issued by police in 1992 has been on display at local businesses in Springfield for years.

MISSING

Sherrill Levitt
Age 47

Suzie Streeter
Age 19

Stacy McCall
Age 18

Call Springfield, Missouri Police Department
(417) 864-1700

graduate finish a course of study in a school and receive a diploma

suspect someone who may be responsible for a crime

25

Amsterdam diamond heist

On 25 February 2005, a daring diamond heist took place at Schiphol Airport in Amsterdam. Two men dressed as employees of the Dutch airline KLM arrived at the cargo terminal. But they weren't employees. They arrived in a stolen KLM car. The men then stopped a lorry near a runway. It was driving up to a KLM aeroplane. The lorry was carrying millions of pounds worth of diamonds.

The robbery was clever because it was so simple. The lorry carrying the diamonds had two drivers. The armed thieves stopped the lorry and forced the two drivers to lie face down on the ground. Many people were watching as this happened. But the robbery went so quickly that no one could stop it. The thieves got in the lorry and casually drove off with the diamonds.

The final price tag for this infamous European heist was around £75 million. That makes it the world's biggest diamond robbery.

Schiphol Amsterdam

Security

The security at Schiphol Airport was surprisingly relaxed. Two weeks before the robbery, four men stole a KLM cargo lorry and uniforms. This theft allowed the men to move around in secure areas of the airport and even practise their robbery. No one realized this was happening until after the crime.

Any suspects?

The thieves have not been seen since. Their lorry was later found, but the thieves and the diamonds were gone. The type of diamonds stolen made it harder to track them. Many of the diamonds were **uncut**. These types of diamond are much harder to track than cut diamonds because there are fewer records of them. The thieves could easily pass them off as newly discovered diamonds to diamond buyers.

uncut diamonds

History's unsolved crimes

Nothing stirs the imagination quite like unsolved crimes. Huge sums of money, stolen works of art and mysterious disappearances capture people's interest. Police and other authorities work hard to crack these cases. Is Dan Cooper still alive somewhere? Was the Provisional IRA involved in the 2004 Northern Bank robbery in Belfast? Where are the diamonds that were stolen in Amsterdam in 2005? Such questions might never be answered.

Glossary

alias false name, especially one used by a criminal

associate person you spend time with or work with

elude escape or get away from someone

fragile delicate or easily damaged

graduate finish a course of study in a school and receive a diploma

heist armed robbery

hijack take illegal control of a vehicle, such as an aeroplane

hostage person held against his or her will

identity who a person is

loot stolen money or valuables

mastermind person who plans and controls the way an action is carried out

ransom money or objects that are demanded in order to set free someone who is being held captive

serial number number that identifies a product, such as money or an appliance

suspect someone who may be responsible for a crime

tamper interfere with something so that it becomes damaged or broken

uncut not shaped by cutting, especially precious stones or diamonds

vault room or compartment for keeping money and other valuables safe

walkie-talkie radio that is held in the hand, powered by batteries and used to communicate over short distances

Books

Crime-Fighting Devices (Sci-Hi: Science and Technology), Robert Sneddon (Raintree, 2012)

Great Art Thefts (Treasure Hunters), Charlotte Guillain (Raintree, 2013)

Unsolved Robberies (Project X), John Malam (Oxford University Press, 2014)

Websites

www.fbi.gov/fun-games/kids/kids
Learn more about the Federal Bureau of Investigation, safety tips and go on an FBI adventure on this website.

www.gardnermuseum.org/resources/theft
Find out more about this daring museum theft, and see for yourself the beautiful works of art that have yet to be recovered.

Index

art 15, 16, 17, 29

Cooper, Dan 6, 7, 8, 9, 29

diamonds 18, 26, 28, 29

Federal Bureau of Investigation (FBI) 8, 9, 16

heists 10, 12, 26
hijackings 6, 7, 9
hostages 10, 12

investigators 7, 8
Isabella Stewart Gardner Museum 15, 16, 17

jewellery 18, 21

Kellerman, Mary 22
kidnappings 12, 24

Levitt, Sherrill 24
Lloyds Bank 18, 19, 20, 21

McCall, Stacy 24
McMullan, Kevin 10, 12
money 7, 8, 9, 16, 18, 19, 22, 23, 26, 29

Northern Bank 10, 11, 12, 13, 29

paintings 15, 16
poisonings 22, 23
Provisional Irish Republican Army (IRA) 12, 29

Rembrandt 15
robberies 10, 12, 13, 18, 19, 20, 21, 26, 29

safe deposit boxes 18, 21
Schiphol Airport 26, 29
skulls 9
Streeter, Suzanne 24
suspects 23, 24

vaults 10, 13
Vermeer 15

Ward, Chris 10, 13